# The Subsequent Blues

# The Subsequent Blues

Gary Copeland Lilley

Four Way Books
New York City

Distributed by
University Press of New England
Hanover and London

Editorial Office
Four Way Books
POB 535, Village Station
New York, NY 10014
www.fourwaybooks.com

Library of Congress Catalogue Card Number: 2002116855

ISBN 1-884800-54-8

Cover art: *When the Sun Goes Down*
by Gary Copeland Lilley,
Silvertone Guitar, collage, paint, handmade charms and fetishes.
December 2002.

Cover art photo by Suzy Poling
Cover design by Christian Acker for Cubanica

This book is manufactured in the United States of America and printed on acid-free paper.

 Publication of this book is made possible in part by an award from the National Endowment for the Arts, which believes that a great nation deserves great art, and by a generous grant from a private foundation

NATIONAL
ENDOWMENT
FOR THE ARTS

Four Way Books is a division of Friends of Writers, Inc., a Vermont-based not-for-profit organization. We are grateful for the assistance we receive from individual donors and larger foundations.

Distributed by University Press of New England
One Court Street, Lebanon, NH 03766

# ACKNOWLEDGMENTS

I wish to show my appreciation to the editors of the magazines in which some of the poems in this collection first appeared:

*32 Poems*: "Riding with the Dragon"

*88*: "Prayer to Saint James Byrd of Jasper Texas"

*The African American Review*: "Voyeur"

*The Bridge*: "Divining the Intersection of Automobile and Dog" and "The Ride From Ellington Bridge"

*Drum Voices Revue*: "Who Sez Thunderbirds Can't Fly," and "King Elijah's Directions to the Graveyard"

The poems "Sanctuaries for the Deacon's Sons," and "High Point," first appeared in the anthology, *Cabin Fever*, Word Works Press, 2003.

The poem "Who Sez Thunderbirds Can't Fly," appeared in the anthology, *Beyond the Frontier*, Black Classics Press, 2002.

I want to thank The Washington D.C. Commission on the Arts and The National Endowment for the Arts for the support of fellowships for poetry that made much of this work possible.

I thank E. Ethelbert Miller for again and again stepping up like some kind of lone ranger, and for his infectious passion for poetry.

A shout of thanks in the appreciation for the discussions, the workshopping, and so much more, to good friends Ernesto Mercer and Monica Slade.

I wish to express my thanks to Keith and Heloise Wilson for the right touch at the time, for the important push. I'm also thankful for the entire Warren Wilson College MFA Program, for being such a community for writers. I've grown in the continuing friendship of Adrian Blevins, Amelia Cox, Patrick Donnelly, Robert Thomas, and Van Jordan. In particular, I am grateful to my teachers Joan Aleshire, Betty Adcock, Laura Kasischke, and Eleanor Wilner, who have given me a writing life. Tony Hoagland is in here, too, for his D.C. workshop as well, and beyond.

This publication is made possible with a regrant from the Council of Literary Magazines and Presses, supported by public funds from the New York State Council on the Arts, a state agency.

For my mother
Lillian Camilla Copeland Lilley

# TABLE OF CONTENTS

I

# Prelude to the Predicament

Ain't you the image, a part of the creator,
when you got love growing in the garden
ain't everything raised in its warmth,
asked the snake.

Thickets grew in the path,
air beneath the trees fouled
and birds shied to the sky.
Wolves howled behind
the red of their teeth,
vultures reversed their spiral
and discovered a taste for death.

Weeping fell like stones.

A saxophone wind, the first low notes,
wailed the story of troubles forever.
They ran, mouths wide open,
eyes pinpointed and seeing nothing
but ground moving backwards
under their flying feet.

## RITUAL OF THE BUSH
*Winston-Salem, 1970*

The bushmen gather every morning
their eight track louder than traffic
one block south of the high school
disturbing everybody with the proof
that the army didn't draft undesirables.

Blue jeans and boots and sometimes a black
leather jacket. Most of them are Panthers.
Nappy heads jailhouse tattoos and Jimi Hendrix.
Boys gone bad and Ford the darkest one
the sun above his head is nothing more

than his reflection.  Lidded eyes a scrim
of marijuana smoke he blazes a good morning
to a school girl "I might die tonight baby
but if you want my love today's okay."
She doesn't stop puts an extra switch
in her walk and crosses on the red.

The bushmen laugh like a shake of dice
to the twirl of her ass and beautiful
barefaced lack of mercy.
They spike the joke with a bottle of 'Bird.

It's almost empty when it gets to Ford
and in this moment in the shade
he knows they'll repeat what he said
like a proverb all day.

4

# SANCTUARIES FOR THE DEACON'S SONS

This is the poem where my brother becomes
me in the pulpit at his Pentecostal church
and the faithful lean forward in their seats
as he witnesses having been a womanizer,
a liar, a cocaine thief and nothing
could touch him, how he'd laid on the side
of a lean shot glass until late in the day
with God over him, how he jack-hammered
holes in the crazy streets, bandana dripping
and him pushing the blade, how the summer
was the heat, and trouble and love simmered
to a circumstance, getting sanctified strength
in lockdown, the right shoes to walk parole
and the blues, Lucifer playing the steel strings.

# ORACLE AT THE END OF THE BAR

I'm drinking Jim Beam doing small sips
in the sentences no one interrupts.
You talk to yourself nobody's got a damn
word to waste on whatever you have to say.
Stools lined with government workers.
This fast crowd of mortgages drinks
and it turns a moon of consequences.
Leon who beats his wife will get jacked
leaving this bar about 3AM he will wear
her bruises tonight. Johnny Cole
a nostalgic pimp in shades walks in
just so people know he's not dead.
The cash and carry boys roll through
'cause money gets off the street
to watch a piece of the game.
Lil' Nate will get shot in the foot
for his jacket and will get a job
when he gets off crutches.
Dorothy rides bottles in the mirror
knowing she's the prettiest
crackhead in the room her man John
is hustling just so she doesn't
have to sell some ass. She will
hit the bricks John is going down tonight
on possession with intent. Herm's holding on
to a  quarter and a dime. Lynne's going home
and will arrive in time for the booty-call.
The cop's daughter Elizabeth will leave
with the cash and carry crew
and for a few hours more she's free.
Outside in the light that comes
from the bar there's a man

begging cigarettes and he looks right
into your eyes. You can believe
that Leon's early morning stagger
will be just the chance he needs.

# Rudeboy in the Light

Anthawn sits loose on the couch in big clothes.
Black jeans hang off his hips and collect
at his feet like pools, the run-off cascading
over his size twelve boots. A red double-X shirt
falls off his shoulders and covers the bone
of his chest.  Long arms lost in the sleeves, both
hands busy on the gun.  He's got a pantheon
of stashed steel gods but this particular piece
he knows is new, stolen still in the box.
A pimp-flash that must be seen, the persuader
with no bodies yet is a beautiful burner.
The stainless barrel as he wipes it down
with the silicone cloth holds him like a mirror.

# OUR LADY OF THE BIRDS

14th Street, the gentrified give a wide berth
to her prayers.  Her dirt is offensive
and all the pigeons seem diseased.

She's old, the color of dust-covered patent leather,
layers of bad smelling clothes
hang off her thin body.  Her gray hair is cut close.

At the House of Ruth, the shelter for women,
some sit outside with the bruises and a look I've seen
in my mother's kitchen.  The stare of her marriage

before she put the knife in her husband's chest
and left him to drive himself to the hospital, ending
the beatings, after eighteen years of them.

He drove past woods and fields, the knife handle
in his peripheral vision, the blade cutting a little every time
he turned the wheel to Mercy.

Said he was lucky the blade missed his heart,
only thing that kept him from passing out and dying
beside the road was to focus on all those birds

flying past the windshield. Every afternoon
the old lady tosses seeds, the pigeons gather
at her different sized and colored shoes.

The bruised women watch from the yard
as the old lady raises her arms
and the birds rise like prayers in her hands.

# The Autobiography of Marcella Ricks

I was intending to stay up the road north
where I've done about everything
from domestic work to owning
my beauty shop.  I came back after I buried
my Mama.  I didn't think that being in her house
would keep me from wanting to get away
from the flies and fields and crazy Negroes
of Sandy Cross but that's the way
I guess God plans it.

Everything starts with my mama, Daisy Morris
who heated water for laundry and shelled peas.
Old time hymns steeping in her kitchen
she was our church right here stirring her pots.
The grace in the morning when some fools
stole her firewood.  We all chipped in
and got a gas stove she didn't really want.
Said, a good cook fire starts with kindling and keeps
the kitchen warm.  She wanted this house
to be a place for any of the family
lost, sick, or tired that might come home.

I graduated from the High School for the Negroes
in 1956.  Only girl in the family and the first
one of us to do so.  My grandfather was still alive
but the farm wore him down till nothing was left
to give the land but soul.  He took off his troubles
like a hat, always hung them outside his door.
My Mama, his oldest daughter.  He'd given her
the big portion of woodland, a blacker dirt
than his fields held.  Her sister ballpoint penned
a nasty note on a brown paper bag

so greasy you could see clear through it,
and Mama never again put foot past garden's line.
She said nothing is bigger than family.

The eighty acres behind her house,
my brothers claimed they didn't know
the taxes came due.
A white man owns it now.

Before my mother passed she stayed with me.
Those short last years I believe she was happy.
My youngest brother would weep, his heart
a lonely holiday whenever he saw her photograph
or heard someone speak her name.
I told him nigger please, I hope don't nobody
be that kind of fool for me.

Mama's joke was if there could be a time
not one person in this family
would take a drink, please good Lord
when she's laid to rest let it be that day—
most of the family shook
from sun-up to dark.

I've had two husbands
and loved them both.
All four of my children
can drive you crazy
but I got a whole carload
of precious grands.

Now I'm back here where my father's a story,

he left my mother and the six of us.  A yellow man
with booze bad eyes, the sweetest Johnny
for miles around.  Took time and sugar
to slow him down.  The last week of his life
saw another amputated limb.  Keep your hand
in God's was her prayer, so one day I'd be able
to forgive him, and I've lived by that
the best I can.

## ASKARI'S FLOW, THE FREE STYLE
*for M'Wile Yaw Askari, DC jazz poet, 1947 - 2000*

First believe there are no plans,
that most of life is improv
and there was no anticipating
his next step, take the walking stick
and then start on the east edge
where Florida Avenue turns
into U Street at the cross of Seventh,
where he grieved the marriage
of bullet and man of peace,
the book of matches and gasoline
in the last summer of negroes,
and some of the looted stores
are now afro-centric shops
among the curry and rice and peas
of West Indian restaurants,
graybeard Rastas chant down Babylon
smoking ganga, stirring the pots,
where Baba is the blessing
that only righteous men are given,
past Popeye's spicy wings
and the cheap synthetic wigs,
his shoulder bag of incense and oils,
meditations and five dollar poems
sold on the retail side of the street,
and let's not forget the thief years
cooling in Lorton Prison, or returning
clean and alone from left coast
drug time, beepers and cell phones,
the greasy sandwich, the diabetes
that put the sugar in his hands
so bad he couldn't wash his head,
the third-world barber shop

where they cut the locks,
a throne reserved for players,
M'wile's place, where the robes
of the griot are patched
the hustle had better be smooth
and worthy of this African
who'd never expect
that for him so many
people would mourn.

# ALL THAT LAZARUS JAZZ

All you twice-slapped saints
in the street dressed in black,
his family's taking it hard.
He was sick they said, but now
he three days dead,
you guys are just too late.
I've got the blessing game,
around here I'm the man.
I take pawn on crowns
and solid gold rings
so go ahead Jesus, I'll church
up the change, you do
that water to wine thing.
Lazarus has gone.
He's in the grave, they say
he is no more, you guys
are just too late.
I made a mojo bag,
took dust from his tomb,
I've burned sage and cedar
in every room of his home.
Yes I've fed the black cat
and polished my wishbone,
had the crooked-teeth conjurer
look into my palm.
I played my lucky number
late last night and hit
five dollars on it straight.
I'll bet you slapped suckers
all of that, 'cause I
have faith
in blood.

# KING ELIJAH GIVES KEISHA THE RECIPE TO GET RID OF ROBERT

Look through your basket of laundry
cut a piece of your husband's sock
to line the bottom of the mojo bag

start him stepping to the door

write a letter with your prayer/fold it
small/to get things stirring put in two
spoons of dirt from a good woman's grave

for the proper power to carry the message

pour in a bit of ground lemon peel
and five crushed peppercorns to irritate
the passages in his head if he remains

longer than it takes to pack his clothes

to remove fouled love and for peace of mind
add the Queen of the Meadow root
sprinkle some Demon Be Gone perfume

drop some lavender oil at the threshold

and bury the bag in your yard/leave a *ve ve*
of Erzulie close by and then pour some honey
and the man will walk clean out your heart.

# KING ELIJAH'S DIRECTIONS TO THE GRAVEYARD

The sweet musk of plowed dirt, over country
as dark as the chamber of a cold heart
or an oiled pistol.  The melancholy
of whiskey and guitar, a blued steel night.
No moon slash or razor.   There is no star
as good a guide as the tombstone neon
that hangs over the long bar, the half-full glass
where talk swings dry, thin, and quick, and red eye
cigarettes beckon through the haze.  Jukebox
jumps, a saxophone pushes smoke to the ceiling.
A rattle of bullets and ball and chain,
the dust raising dance of hoodoo saints.
A prayer sung like rainfall, and everyone
that you see in there is already gone.

# HOW TO COOK ROAD KILL

I come round the curve
and see the one-eyed pick-up leave
then the deer knocked
half in the ditch just before dawn
a spike buck dead and warm
to the touch not a mark so I knew
he might be busted up some
but the end for him was
that long neck turned back
toward the road a black eye examining
frost on the brown grass
the tongue hanging from his mouth.

I'm Henry Knight by the way
that's my red diesel
with my name on the cab
got a sweet girl on the coast
and the road to her glory
doesn't have a mailbox for shame
she knows comforts enough
and really puts out a welcome
you want a woman to act
like she can't live without you
I'll accept most things said
by people who give me work
but my first wife told me
I wasn't even the best
husband she'd had
I told the bitch she could walk
I come back the next
and on the kitchen table
there's one pot

one pan one plate one cup
one knife one fork
one spoon.

So I hang the deer upside down
you gotta cut behind the tendons
splay the hoofs on a short pole
raise it on a pulley in the barn
a hundred pounds
he dressed out easy
all the ribs were broken
but the tenderloin was lean
leave a small completion of fat
to game up the garlic
and onions in a skillet
while you let the liver
and heart soak
in a pail of salt and water.

# THE PENTECOSTAL MINISTER

pays bills for a rehab house out of profits
from his janitor business, not the love offering
given as the band of sanctified boys in shades
play the gospel and drums.  The congregation
ghosting up the dollars.  A church of women
holy with the chorus, and him thinking about
the twelve men recovering in the house,
some sitting on the porch fragile and clean
watching the familiar action in the drug hole
across the street.  He prays to remove temptation
of smoking coke, his brother offers to burn
the place down.  The answer

pure as his white preaching robes, as close
as those stick-up years when he was
what you didn't want to see (cold sweat
beginning above the mask; the pistol, big,
black and steady in his hand).
And after that, it was the terror he'd thrown
into the rook cop who got small behind a tree
and the miracle of Officer Cooke rising
the right-side rib cage blown out
through the tight fit of desk riding blues.

Then it was his turn under the gun:
nightsticks, boots, pepper spray,
and seven years of brown clothes,
the last three on chain.  Black men,
bush hooks and sling blades
walking in Carolina ditches.  And him holding
together while a cottonmouth crawled
between his feet.  The road gang days,

no sudden moves, he learned to trust
the snake.

He stayed calm those years of Sundays
turning his memories like the worn cards
.that find the way into the joint
as fast as the bible; loading cases
of white liquor into the semi,
pan bread and blackstrap molasses
on the kitchen table, getting kissed
in a Mercury Comet, riding Lowground Road
to hunt with and play ball against the cousins,
the revival and the baptism, the smell of fish
from the river, the wading into
a saved gray morning.

The grandmothers with tambourines
are saints driving the rhythm,
the congregation in high spirits
sweating creases from their clothes,
he cuts into a dance
before the altar, grabs the mike
and the band rides with it,
*Keep your lamp trimmed and burning*
*See what the Lord has done*
*Keep your lamp trimmed and burning*
*Our troubles are almost gone.*

# THE NEW RESIDENT PROSTITUTE

has more teeth in her smile than the last one
(who at a hard-lived forty had her heart stop).
She's got a blonde dye job that doesn't reach
her Maryland roots, a spot of rouge
the street life on her cheeks. Above each eye
a turquoise strip runs into the creases.
When she first turned up beside the underpass
last year, in sight of the Capitol's dome,
she was a white spot waiting with the rest
for Boneman and the smack to come down.

Check her stroll, a loose tee shirt cut below
the tit ribs and denim shorts showing the promise.
Her legs spotted with blue heroin hooker bruises
doing a slow dance in the clap of strapless sandals.
Her head thrown back because everyone knows
hard pimps and players will allow an older woman
a trade in the cracks of their neighborhood,
let her work a living in alleys and cars parked
at the boundaries where rock whores beam,
and the hoochies and churchwomen walk.

And now she's headed to Lou's, the greasiest spoon
still standing after the riots, to gather herself
for the morning hours. She don't much run
her lipsticked mouth, and there's nothing in there
fit to eat, but she always lets Lou know he brews
a good fucking cup of coffee. She looks every man
at the counter in the face and angles
her crossed legs toward the door. She always has
her own pack of cigarettes, her own light,
and anything else that makes it through.

# Let the Devil First Ask One Question

I'm fucking ancient, and I hope I don't look it, but
I used to roll back in the day with the Zealots.
Most of your chosen were bush-head boys. I hate
to say this because it seems like I should be creaking,
I've kissed their mothers and their great-grands.
Ahh, the best lives I've had have been with women
who've died pretty, may they rest at the foot of my throne.
I've been blessed by young ones. For instance, Salome was 17,
but Lilith, she was always 40. I was smoother back then,
I liked older women. Time is nothing, what makes it hard
is the mature sweeties seem saintly now. And I am not.
All the best you see, you've taken. Those who step to me,
I don't chase them. I don't mind at all bumping into some
of your super ladies. Let me guess, that tattooed woman
you have in mind, yes, Magdalene, isn't she just past 20?

23

# There I Was Walking the Therapeutic Mile

Change, the price of a pack of cigarettes
in my pocket the only thing I can
think about Jesse Helms is the fact that
in-state smokes cost less than 3 dollars:
half-hour on a ghost of the plantation.
Cropped out tobacco fields, that filter tip
dangling in the corner crack of my mouth.
I need a phone card.  A freight train of wind
comes through and, I know I'll need a good set
of winter clothes, a hat. Then the rain starts
a quarter mile from the store, three hundred
miles from the Senator. Not much shoulder
to walk on, it's down to ditch or the road
and confederate flags, cars whistling past.

# IF YOU'RE LOOKING IN THE WOODS FOR LEGBA

The holly, dogwood (holy,
crucifixion) or huckleberry tree

(gaming and luck)
is where you go to meet

the big black man (a parade
of animals will precede)

who can teach you
what you want to know.

Have a rooster with you,
turn him loose in the woods (blood

the base of the tree).
You'll find some trouble there,

a storm or high winds
(the dark cloud is him),

continue the song (136th Psalm)
where every verse ends

with the same words (*for his mercy
endureth forever*). Leave a silver coin.

II

# THE PARABLE OF NOT PAYING PROPER TITHES
# PART 1

Pearlie went to King Elijah the root-man
to get a lucky hand. Said his house was full
of the kind of people who wouldn't look
you in the face around 3AM, and cars from New York,
Philadelphia, and Washington were parked idling
along his road. She hit the number six days straight
and never gave him one dime. King Elijah told her mother
that Pearlie should come by and pay him some respect,
that he knew she'd been hitting and won a lot of money.
Pearlie said, What? she ain't got no reason to think
that any of that had anything to do with him. It's her luck
that was winning the money. Cause that's how it is,
everyone gets a lucky run sometime and maybe
this was just her turn.

# THE PARABLE OF NOT PAYING PROPER TITHES
## PART 2

The numbers are played the old way in High Point,
played like they were when Washington Street
was long cars with fins and predatory grills, heroin
in glassine envelopes, and almost every man
wore a brim broke down nasty on the side of his head.
You wrote your digits and your bet in the receipt book.
You kept the carbon to prove the hit and presented it
the next day at the candy store to get paid.
Mustaches were razored sharp.  The young girls
wore tubes and short skirts.  Everyone stood on platforms
and nobody has ever been as slick as King Elijah
when he used to collect the numbers and nods.

# THE PARABLE OF NOT PAYING PROPER TITHES
## PART 3

The seventh day, the day after she rebuked the root man,
Pearlie played and hit for twenty-five hundred
and couldn't find the ticket. She cleaned her entire house
looking for it, turned every pocket in her closet.
She was so desperate sick she'd even checked her fridge.
Went through her garbage piece by piece, more wretched
as she neared the bottom of each bag of pampers,
last week's leftovers, dead soldiers of bourbon
and crushed beer cans. Mouth full of turbulent prayers
she cried in the middle of the scattered trash
when all that was needed was to take King Elijah
some money, a bottle of whiskey
and her sincere apology.

# THE BEAUTICIAN

Ruby fixes the hair of the dead
at night when she closes her salon,
the straightening combs and curlers
in the cold room at the funeral parlor.

At night when she closes her salon,
she drinks and smokes alone.
In the cold room at the funeral parlor
she prays for every customer.

She drinks and smokes alone.
At her mother's bar and grill
she prays for every customer
and waits for the shot and a beer.

At her mother's bar and grill
old ladies remember all their friends
and wait for the shot and a beer
knowing Ruby will style the hair.

Old ladies remember all their friends.
Each one wearing the dark dress
knowing Ruby will style the hair.
Some people say her touch is a blessing.

Each one wearing the dark dress
waiting their turn in her salon.
Some people say her touch is a blessing,
so much sorrow has been in her hands.

Waiting their turn in her salon,
the straightening combs and curlers,
so much sorrow has been in her hands.
Ruby fixes the hair of the dead.

# LOOKING AT CHERYL'S LOVE

The morning—today it hangs like handcuffs
after the gunfire.  In the soup-kitchen
an update to the minute, prophecies
in each cup of coffee.  Cheryl, head in hand,
her elbow propped on the weathered white sill
of her second floor window.  All the shades
are up, crackheads and cops do a slow dance
in front the joint.  She leans out to look on
her man.  She watches him warm the motor
of a Lincoln limousine.  Everything's
tuned up, good fire, no smoke, legitimate
in his pressed black chauffeur suit.  She watches
him, in the squad car's terrible blue lights,
looking at her as he pulls from the curb.

34

## So I Come Back and Find that Now She's Taken the TV

That black and white set on loan so long
it was mostly mine.  A grateful receiver
of all gifts probably cause I'm southern
and was living in three hundred square feet
of studio when she told me to take it
'cause I had nothing else but window and wall.
She knows, I like the small homicide of Friday night.
But it's funny, when some people see you down once
they never can see you as anything but.
I've had four broken noses.  Played street-ball
and fought in bars before both turned deadly—
nothing kills a dream faster than a pistol.
Nothing unplugs you like a woman who feels
you did her wrong, and that's regardless of the proof
of the bourbon you submerge into the draft.

A Russian submarine sits on the arctic shelf tonight,
within reach now only of God.  The poor bastards
have been sacrificed for the secrecy of ordnance
and equipment.  I shot expert with the forty-five,
ready to repel all boarders, kill any invaders,
go ballistic fuck the world from my submarine.
Couldn't wait to play the games with the Russians,
shaking Ivan before going out on patrol.  Loaded
with cigarettes, a war chest of porn, a few bibles,
weight lifting gloves and steel toe boots.

This was my bubblehead prayer prior to going to sea:
    *May the number of surfaces equal the dives.*
    *May the number of surfaces equal the dives.*
    *May the number of surfaces equal the dives.*
Big black American submarine.  We didn't do TV.

We didn't watch it unless
we were home, maybe in the afterglow
in some woman's arms.  But tonight
nothing goes deeper to the man
than living inside the machine, and
I'm contemplating the loss of air, stuck
beneath the thermals, in the damned
thinness, in the cold
lack of time.

# For Sergeant Daniel Anderson, Airborne

Falling through the sky even an eagle
is diminished nearing the earth.

I can see you in Boston Commons
sitting on the wall, telling this story
while the ballerinas smoke, the night after
we got drunk in the last tit bar,
where you dropped hundreds on the two
strippers we liked the most, it was
conversation you were after.
                    You said, the desert
had probably long stripped the cigarette
from the Iraqi's smile.  That blackened skull
on the one-road retreat, a dead man
in a jeep, and how you watched an asshole
in American fatigues fit the filter between
the skull's teeth, how the mocking
of this soldier's death
troubled you all the way
to South America,
                    and now 'troop,
friend, you too are gone.  You decided
the day to leave.  When the news came
my woman said it was guilt
at the things you'd done
(I already knew by then that everything
I'd had with her was finished).
                    She believes all ex-soldiers
should carry a load of shame, she
doesn't understand.  The warrior way
is the making of a saint and what fills
the silk chute is the fierce

breath of God.  The redemption
in a soldier's life is to save a life.
I lit a cigarette and told her

it was probably sadness
over something you'd seen.

# A SACRAMENT FOR THE EGUN

Love, all I ever wanted out of life
I've found in the spirits of the dead.

The deal gone down gets deeper.
Now there are two buildings

full of life-stories someone will tell...
Workers work until they die and then work

from the other side in behalf of their blood.
A white candle on the floor,

a white cup of black coffee,
a cigar, white rum and a clear glass of water

for the ancestors and gods, a page
of a holy book will bring them home.

# The Blind Boys at the 9:30 Club

In the crushed cigarette butts
and sloshed beer on the floor
of the rock and punk hole
skinhead congregants
want music dark and loud
a long way from the gospel.
The opening act
on stage during six decades
and now they've got the mass
of those September souls
lifting on a trio of the original voices.
A merge of amazing grace
and the house of the rising sun
hands white and black
are raised a prayer
begins in the darkness.
The gothic bartenders are busy
serving spirits and the tips
are heavier than they've been
on any other Thursday night
even the tee-shirted
rat-muscled bouncers
relax just a bit.

# THE KING OF THE ONE-LEGGED ASS KICKERS

The old man got pissed, threw a boot
through a window when his wife said
he needed to slow his peg, that he'd stepped
out on her and his kids long before
the sugar changed his dance.
He never understood the oldest boy's anger,
watching him put time shining that left shoe
and knowing the king would be leaving home
creating nights that he'd hear about in school
and then have to fight some older boy,
about somebody's sister who'd went off
with the old man, pulling from
his bottle after cutting with the crutch
a dirty dance on the dusty floor of a juke.
Other men's daughters were marked
with yellow babies by him.  Bastards,
like his gold tooth begging for a beating.
If he was thunder that crooked smile
the lightning flash, the glint of a knife.
Husbands, healing scars and gun wounds
swore that killing the roaming man
who couldn't run would be a second joy
to messing up that half-white face.
His wife fed her kids, took in laundry,
pressed shirts and sheets, flat irons heated
on top the pot belly stove, the grips
wrapped in red flannel to protect her
from burns.  She always kept the door
unlocked for him, never knew another man.
She didn't allow a hard word about him
from anyone in the house but her,
and when she died, in respect

the children still would not cuss him.
In the veterans' hospital, years later,
they took the left leg and he went out
alone. The oldest boy quiet, sober,
sitting right there in the room.

# TOAST TO PAUL THE CAT, DRUGGED IN

Being doped up was one thing
but when he drank
his breath stank.  Standing in the door
of the Hillcrest, his foul mouth
up in everybody's face,
half bottle of slosh in his hand
breaking the only real rule
of the establishment.

Every song's got a bag of blue notes
he'd say when he played the piano
in the dark auditorium
after football practice in tenth grade.
Our running back, cuss words,
quick moves and cuts
scatting across the keys.

Came from the Joppa crowd,
canonized, drinking the life-
blood of Jesus.  A cold beer
sweating in the can
the year he dropped out,
got a misdemeanor drunk
and ninety days
in the population playing
the rhyme and a game of cards.

He grew tall and hustled pool,
the nine ball in the diamond
of solids and stripes. Beating
factory men with the bank
on pay day nights, catching them

with 45 malt and shit talk
before they got home, letting them
each write their own tickets,
adding up their cigarettes lit
and not smoked,
burning on the rails of the table.

When we turned nineteen
we went up the coast
to Wildwood, New Jersey,
to bad girls that were good,
and weed that was better.
He went to hang out
before the draft.  I had
a student deferment
and tossed bones
that whole summer.

And now I'm nineteen years
on my post office job
doing a street box route,
and I see him
in the ragged morning
looking into a crack boy's hand

and later we talk through
the judgments
of our divorces
and near misses, estranged kids,
the loss of wisdom teeth,
his jungle rush
of long range recon,

the pure lawlessness
that rules the bush.

Says he's a boonie-rat.
The unit called him Bama,
knowing damn well
that he's from North Carolina.
It was the drawl, he said,
and maybe those blues
he mail-ordered
from Randy's record shop.

Might-a-been, he says,
the way he strolled
with his weapon, second-
naturedly blending into mud,
he just loved being
alive one step from death
walking on the point.

In The Hillcrest he sees me
and nobody else
and knows
I'll buy his next drink
so he smoothes out two dollars
and plays Jimmy Reed.
And for six jumping songs
of roadhouse piano
he's catching passes,
he on the dance floor,
he's the boogaloo,
he's still the hero after the game.

# My Head is a Mojo Bag

Unlit candles on both sides.  The altar,
the dog skull wired to a hubcap in the middle
of the rusting springs.  *Ogun's Bed*,
an art installation with tools and blades
on a green pick-up going to New York.
The trip barely started and weather was worse
inside the truck, the rain of an entire winter
in one freezing night, and she probably couldn't
tell you any better than I where we missed the detour
in all this, and I lit a cigarette.  She doesn't smoke.
My nerves a dragging pipe and the premonition
of the next five hours north on a slippery road.
She's got the wheel, everything is a target.
Lethal from any chamber of her heart,
she's the dum-dum load.  I tossed the smoke
through the open back window between us
leaving the tunnel in Baltimore.  It rolled
along the hubcap filter first to the dog's snarl.
The trucker pushing a two trailer rig behind us
hit his horn, a long blues howl, and moved into
the fast lane, the god of iron washing us down
with highway grime until his lights were gone.

46

# Putting the Match to the Cigarette

Black coffee at the diner, the expected ghost
is the empty stool beside me, your ghost.

Dark tide, the moon a lingering kiss, your lips,
the sea salt, my glass of water is the ghost.

I see lovers holding hands haunting the same
gray streets I walk at night, smoking with your ghost.

Who knows if you ever find this kind of love
again. Behind the door like luggage, a ghost.

Laid out, my bible of longing, the blue suit
I wear on weekends, a consignment store ghost.

The break of morning, on my side of the bed
attending my marks and tattoos is a ghost.

Your hand moves on my frame, across an old scar,
the cut lily in a vase, another ghost.

## DIVINING THE INTERSECTION
## OF AUTOMOBILE AND DOG

So Ernesto and me step out of Irene's studio
to sit on her stoop and fire up.  She's upstairs
putting a quilt of blades, chains, gun frames,
and tools to Ogun's iron bed. Each twisting tie
of wire to her piece of art cuts a blood hymn
to the warrior god. A dog's skull sits in middle
of the rust. These warrior times, this gathering

of axes and knives call for an offering of tobacco,
a dog soldier sacrifice. I light up the last jack on me
and ball up the pack because this is my ritual,
the stick of fire hanging in my mouth, the burning story
as good as currency in a shelter or a prison. A man
on the move I don't sit still no longer than a cigarette.

Then down the street comes Kingsbury's son,
Louis, carrying his dead black and white dog.
Spilling a mixed load of cries and cursing, his Jordans
are blood-stained, he's just a boy-ball of scream,
his wails are the skid marks down the street.
He's hugged the pup, a smear of blood is on his face.

All the hustlers stop working. A woman wearing blue
leaves the shade people and takes Louis into her arms.
Today she's Yemaya, comforter of children.
The hustlers lay their hands on the boy and pup.
Ernesto and me, we take long pulls on our smokes
then we go back up to Irene's and she's sitting
with a Cuban cigar in front of Ogun's iron bed.

## THE AUTHORITY OF BURNSIDES' RULE
## IS ON THE ASS-POCKET OF WHISKEY

I've had too much to drink when I'm flirting
with midget Tanya at the club just 'cause
she's coming at me and she has lovers
stacked up in here who are mad about that fact
like James who's standing against the far wall
arms crossed looking at me with that whose damn
car did he just wash for crack money look
and she leans close and says if I tell you
that I'll be in here next Friday without
my man you gonna put a fantasy
in my head and I say I'm trying hard
to get past the fantasy you putting
in mine and I unscrew myself leaving
a shot of bourbon untouched on the bar

# OFFERING TO OSHUN AT THE 55 CLUB

This is about nothing but the want:
a basket of wings/extra hot sauce
a pitcher of light beer/and standing
in front of the stage/sliding a five
up her inner thigh
toward the yellow garter/close enough
to kiss her ass/she turns
and a heart is in my face
I can smell her sweat/I can
almost taste from the jar of honey.

# VOYEUR

*Ogun is the Yoruba god of iron, he retreats deep into the
woods with his shyness. Oshun is the Yoruba goddess of
love and beauty, sweetwaters, enticements.*


The woods, in the morning;
when mist rises from lowground
the earth is breathing
it pulls at the boots
and makes walking slow.
Still dark, the trees drip with dew.

The underbrush pushes
against his thighs, water runs
in his jeans. Ogun walks
off the path and the fall of his foot
sounds like a grunt offered up,
response to the call of the trees.

A ritual of wanting, a spark
of lust illuminating a side of himself
he has not seen. Oshun moves
toward him from some far corner
a recurring dream, a blues heard best
within the heart. Anything asleep
she awakes. The night and stars
burn when she touches him.

This morning he crept to the edge
of the woods and sat on a familiar stump
behind the honeysuckle covered bush.
His line of sight from sweet scent
into the clearing
and on the back of Oshun's house.

The house is sturdy board
washed by rain and rubbed
by wind to a warm smoky mood.
A dress of stones and gems
bared at the foundations
where weather touches ground.
At her windows there are no shades
to hide the inside. He reached
into his pocket seeking smoke deep
to the seam. He cupped his hand
and struck the flame.

He imagines her reaching into the globe
and lighting her lamp, the wick burning
trim and neat, a reservoir of scented oil.

She comes to the back porch
in her yellow robe, at the long-handle
and sets before the mouth
an empty porcelain pitcher,
to prime the pump, a mason jar of water.
She begins the strokes
that pull life from the soil.
It spills off the pump stand
and into a lace of weed flowers,
the spot of tall grass
where the water has been before.

The ashes fall from his cigarette
and into the cuff of his jeans.
Ogun opens up his work-shirt
in the expanding morning heat.

He tosses the burning end
into the wet honeysuckle leaves
and when he steps into the yard
his steps are steady as the water
dripping from Oshun's porch.

III

# Who Sez Thunderbirds Can't Fly

The streetlamp's glow slashed into my room
across the bed the books
the daily news and clothes piled on top
across an empty jack bottle
and into my full face the malignancy of light

I own the night and who sez
thunderbirds can't fly

I'm driving to my domain
a bar thick with blues
and I'm the guy you're looking for
if you want to do anything

you can step to me

Come past the old man
and the proof of his repentance
past whatever mercy surrounds him
that iridescence of gasoline
a heavy rain can't wash away
it's kind of beautiful
when you see it as I do
I see people hard-walkers all
doing what they need
and surviving

Come past old Nairobi
a prophet who says he knows
the secret in the progression of days
and figuring your taxes
from the number of locks

securing your door

Nairobi's always piss drunk
and pissed off
sleeping in the cemetery
I think he's an obituary
postdated

And his point is
aren't we all

cause the soul dies first
from being hard all the time
trust in God and you better
believe in Satan taking what he can
while he's free and what else is it
that keeps us here so damned
and so alive but the music
between those two so crank it up
sit back rudeboy style
light a cigarette and ride

# HITTING IT AT THE PARADISE APARTMENTS

Mike Cross, who'd had the clap so much lately
we started calling him Applause, left his dope
on the nightstand and is in the bathroom
sweating through a piss.  Once Mike was known
as Red Cross cause he wanted to give
CPR, breathe this place back into a corner boy
who'd been shot on his doorstep up close
by a Columbian. We'd listened to
the argument.  Loco-Ramon was right,
dude was gone like the single gunshot,
his life bouncing like a basketball
off alley bricks and the lean shadows,
all the Illegals, got lost in the sirens
and we'd bailed, no talk, to the Carry-Out.

Down-Town, who was once a real basketball
player, could hold his own against the boys
from the college teams who summer leagued us
to second tier ballers. A streak shooter
who'd take us up, corner boys who played strong
fundamentals (if Mike Cross can only
go to his right, only give him the ball
when he goes to his right). Down-Town
is in this heat wearing three layers of clothes
looking like he'll snitch for a spot in the shelter.
I smoke a gem through a can, a pin-punched bed
of cigarette ash, clean-shaved, pay-check angel
in white shirt and tie, fingering
the shotgun hole like I'm playing a trumpet.

Lisa sits at the back end of a hit
looking in her compact mirror to see

if she's still here.  She's on the other side
of the bed with a wet towel cooling
her glass stem so she can flip the screen and
fire the faded ghost of crack. The small room
is so hot we're both near naked, down to
our boxers, hers are pink with paisley print,
her breasts are now about a mouthful each.
She says if I feel like I want some don't go
to anybody else without coming
to her first, 'cause it looks like her stuff
ain't good if we tight and I don't want it.
So I show respect for her game.

# Blackheart

You can never know a woman

I was in a fast car driving hard
and that one damn thought
was rocking my rat-motor mind

Four-barreling a sweet Chevy south

My candy red Impala Super Sport
rescued from a farmer's barn
parked when his son flew off
to the desert storm

Rally wheels and the dusty windshield
two hundred horses unrestrained
slow drivers getting the hell out the way

I'd been driving three hours heading home
The morning air was cool
a highway hum blew
through the window
that melancholy whine
you can only hear driving alone

Repair work started choking the road
and it began to rain a drawl drizzle
The morning traffic was creeping
through dixie mist
law-abiding citizens seeking
a gas station with a clean bathroom
and styrofoam cups of old coffee

Drivers sitting erect as dicks
everyone locked
into their own red-eyed existence

Construction boys
highway shrapnel
idling in the closed left lane
in their steel-toe shoes and stiff jeans
scratching their asses adjusting their crotches
spitting Redman juice into the gasoline
and oil sheen on the road

I grabbed the bottle of Jack
drank the last corner capped the empty
and shoved it back behind the seat

The sign
two cardinals on a dogwood branch
"Welcome to North Carolina"
(home of Jesse Helms
is fifty years backwards
as the jim crow flies)

I was heading home to figure this shit out:

What's the deal with a woman
who doesn't put herself into a kiss
the most intimate act anyone can do
If she doesn't give herself holy into a kiss
you ain't got beyond the surface

And that's the real sign I'd missed
her kisses
metered out like pocket change
I roared my red car home
and screamed out my open window
I don't know one goddam thing

## (NOT IN THE RAP SHEET OR THE OBITUARY)

Lil' Pete gets tired of arguing with Wilson
about the quality of the dope he'd sold
and Wilson smoked two hours ago,
when he turns to leave.  Wilson unwilling
to see the pocket full of coke he imagines
in Pete's jacket walk away without him,
reaches out a hand to slow Pete's step.
Catching the move from the corner
of his eye, Pete swirls to face him,
hair-triggered Glock already in hand,
coming up the side of Wilson's head.
Wilson's flounder eyes big up fast.
He opens his mouth to make a plea
just as Pete shoots him.  One round between
his left ear and eye.  Wilson collapses
twitching and pissing into the sidewalk.
Lil' Pete stands stiff in that bullet-hole
of silence, in a matter of seconds
he was completely alone.

# Dear Jeffrey, I Don't Care if You're Crazy.

Do you remember your coma
the windshield of the Ford
that ate the red light and you
right out the crosswalk?

You were hooked to machines.
I couldn't imagine that you were down
making me love so much my own life.

Your skull x-rayed and the fractures
looked like constellations
had fixed themselves in your mind.
Safety glass kept working out of your scalp.

We both in a bottle one year later
you said you'd died and came back
so it must've been the devil's hand.
Nothing new about death you said
what fucks you up is life unlived.

Kool and the Gang cars and clothes
I watched you drive the settlement
to whatever spot you sleep in now.

I've eroded and protect myself with tattoos.
What do you do?
Are your voices saviors
and your layers of shirts shields?

Aunt Marcella is dead.
Do you remember younger brother
how she loved you?  Can you

hear me calling from Washington DC.
I live round First and O Street and see
the homeless this is where they eat.
Crazy/drunks a lost tribe roams
from Whitehurst Bridge dry mouth hungry.
A muddy face and I can't guess

how you look now Jeffrey.  Does a woman
sleep next to you?  What of seventeen years gone
will your madness show me?
How many times have you died?

# Report from Marcus, the Hearse Driver for Wilson's Funeral Home

Yall know we buried Stinky today. Some fool
sprayed across the street from the church:
you ain't dead dawg. In the box young and done,
still didn't look old enough to be a drive-by.
And get this, had a big onyx ring on his little finger
and in both ears a diamond stud. These hip-hop
niggaz posing for targets. I'll tell you what,
that black linen suit looked good, I bet
his mother loved him in it. Pair of his boots
hanging in the tree over that crew
drinking forties by Abraham's store.
He would've dug the tears and tight clothes
on those sweet girls he'd kicked it with.
All his love everlasting.
The whole school was there, the student body
crumbling into themselves.
And his boys goddamn
standing there looking tougher than death.

# THE RIDE FROM ELLINGTON BRIDGE

She squeezes room for both
in the overload, apologizes
to everybody's feet he steps on,
gets hard looks as she wipes
the boy's nose. It's early afternoon
and it seems her day
is already too long so she asks,
*Does anybody know what time it is?*

There's no answer coming, everyone
is as silent as me, they look away
to find another CD, they adjust
their headphones, or they smell
under their own armpits
as the bus rolls through the cross
of 14th and U, past the McDonalds,
and the boy, seeing the golden arches,
danced, begged and cried.

He goes off like a burglar alarm
and shrieks all the way to 1st Street.
I see the whole bus turn
a hard shoulder to them.
The wails come from nose and mouth,
all of it boiling down, bubbling
like a thick soup before it burns.

That's when she gets pissed
and pulls him to the door of the bus.
One foot barely touching the floor,
and yes, he recognizes the cadence
of the march, but he still screams.

*Just wait 'til I get you off of here,*
she says, *I'm going to personally feed you*
*a goddamn Happy Meal.*

So maybe she was seeing his daddy's face,
maybe all she'd ever received
was the noise of needless wants,
the consummation of golden lies
from the mouths of men and boys,
but as the bus pulls away
she's slapping her son hard
all across his braided head.

# My Bones Burning Down

Laverne-Laverne is so bad
you say her name twice
she answers the phone
at the Crime Victim's Advocates Office
across from the courthouse

you know if you've seen her before
the human hair weave she flips through
with the salon paint on her nails
those fire engine nights
and golden stars cost some dude

she can't type ten words a minute
'cause she talks to everyone
sitting in the room the shot hustlers
in fresh gear looking to pay
hospital bills and the home-girls
with habits and black eyes
who need a protection order
'cause their baby daddy
still got the keys
and done smoked up
all the money for the rent

you can tell she was raised
on that government cheese
'cause that leopard-skin
mini-skirt ass is real

she stands in the eternity
of those long legs rising
from her fetish of ankle boots

and I can catch her late
at the Nite Cap Bar
'cause she likes a tough guy
with some gin and juice thoughts
and money for the juke
playing her selections
of sweetly-told lies

she's the rollercoaster
checking out your ride
but when she leaves the job
she goes to Wilson's Funeral Home
and gently bathes the elderly
laying on stainless steel trays
and even in that harsh light
she's the hottest damn thing
you'll ever find in a mortuary

# HIGH POINT

When I'm stoned I can see air, thin lines where
parts fit together.  In the dark, my sight
becomes acute, particularly in
the foot of god space surrounding my head.
It's the gift of my age, and my knowing
a lot of dead people.  I moved my life
in boxes in a yellow Ryder truck,
my return to this small town where Coltrane
once lived, loved, and now, there are two crossed streets
that carry his name.  Listening to the jazz
on the gospel station, the horn and all
the min-wage worry, black in a bible
town factory, hard now as it was then.
The last trailer park remains, white only.

# WAITING FOR HARRY

Saturday evening at dusk dark, Miss Nana
who lived in the swallow of longleaf pine
down the lane, was knocking
at my mother's kitchen door. Her voice
was dry leaves blowing through our yard.
I was in my room rocking the radio,
Randy's Records from Memphis Tennessee,
worried about that knock.
Old Sandy Cross women always
needed the nearest fourteen-year-old boy
to cut their firewood on cold nights
and this year it was me.

My mother opened up to the wind. Miss Nana
uncombed hair flying all over her head
was stark sober, crying had left salt trails
in the twist of her face. Her words stumbled
and staggered around her few teeth,
"Yall got to come sit with me while Harry dies."
We followed her to the house down the lane
where Harry's crooked cut at cards
wasn't as sharp as his knife. The peeling paint
on the walls was sooted from the wood stove,

the oil lamps turned down to a soft light.
I knew I wasn't gonna see Barbara Winslow,
a bush hair girl, across the county line
on the other side of this five-mile desert,
the slow song, a phone line of crows,
blue space between notes.
But I was present at the foot
of Harry's naked bed

and saw him leave here loved.
Saw Nana wipe sweat
from above his jaundiced eyes,
down the long scar on his jaw, around
the quick-to-cuss mouth
she'd kissed for fifty years.

# RIDING WITH THE DRAGON

Every fifteen minutes a cigarette flies
from the cab, sparking in the night air stream
on the driver side of the rig.  I'm in the shotgun seat
of a freightliner diesel.  Console between us,
the eight track and a stack of maps, a spilled
carton of Marlboros, one half-empty pack.
I check my old man's profile in the approaching lights,
the sag in his face, an oil-stained ballcap,
the red tip of a cigarette pulling toward his mouth
as he runs the road with his window down.
His left hand on the wheel, right on the stick,
he can drive this steel in his sleep.

# I'm Gonna Live Long
## Unless Something Kills Me

I was the oldest man in the holding cell
the soft gloss on my timbo boots
the loose tongue flapping through
an absence of strings and the way
my beltless baggy jeans sagged
without falling off my waist
because none of that was troubling me
to the hustlers waiting the magistrate
it somehow seemed to say
I'd been there before
but these days the police no longer
allow locked-downs to have cigarettes
and the only time I don't smoke
is when I'm asleep but that's out
of the question so I sit head up
folded securely in my military jacket
and quietly fiend to myself
a pledge not to want a Marlboro
until I make bail and not to eat the baloney
sandwiches handed out by the gap-mouth
trustee who for some reason has a smile
at 4:30AM in the third district jail
I just want to think how my whole night
turned on the blade of a jackknife
from the smile of a short woman
crazy about the unauthorized use
of her in my poems
three drinks deep at the bar
when a brother big as a fridge
and wearing his hat backwards
shows up and starts talking shit
a thick spliff rasta-rolled

for the zig-zag love of the lord
in my pocket hallelujah
there's a prayer to Stagger Lee
the ghetto saint who knows
I ain't got a fair fight left
to give anybody and now
I was the getting the nod of respect
for the *assault with a deadly* charge
and I told the youngens
this shit was all about Art

# PRAYER TO SAINT JAMES BYRD OF JASPER, TEXAS

Sometimes a sufferer wails them church blues.
She's gonna smell gin on my breath, the street
in my clothes. Her good book off the dresser
with the word stronger than the oak, stronger
than the dogwood of the cross. I have worn
misdemeanor green and cleaned right-of-ways
for the state, for a buck-fifty a day.
Where is God? I've run boots into the ground.
Saint James, you kissed your sister at the door
and walked the road. I'm on my hands and knees
in the dry heave dawn wishing one clear eye
to see the way. Saint James take us late night
husbands, brothers, and lost sons safely home.
Lord, rebuke the rollers on their long ride.

# Notes on Poems

### King Elijah Gives Keisha the Recipe to Get Rid of Robert

*Ve Ve*, in Voudou ceremonies and rituals, a symbolic drawing made to summon specific Loas (gods or goddesses).

*Erzulie*, from Voudou (influenced by the Yoruba belief system), is another name for the goddess of feminine sexuality and beauty, and like Oshun is appealed to in matters of the heart.

### If You're Looking in the Woods for Legba

*Legba (Elegba)*, from the Yoruba belief system, is the *loa* (god) of the crossroads, where the spiritual and physical planes intersect. He is the opening to all doors. He's also a trickster.

### A Sacrament for The Egun

*Egun*, from the Yoruba and Congo belief systems, are the spirits of the dead, the ancestors and relations. The term can be applied to singular or plural spirits.

### Toast to Paul the Cat, Drugged In

*Boonie-rat*, term for soldier with highly developed survival skills gained in the bush of Vietnam.

*The point*, the lead man of a military patrol into hostile territory.

### My Head is a Mojo Bag and Voyeur;

*Mojo*, a fetish which contains items considered to have specific magical qualities.

*Ogun*, from the Yoruba belief system, is the Orisha (god) of iron. He is a woodsman, a warrior, and a blacksmith. Symbols of his domain include tools, weapons, and machinery.

THE AUTHORITY OF BURNSIDES' RULE IS ON THE ASS-POCKET OF WHISKEY

*RL Burnside* is a Mississippi hill country bluesman. There are no periods after the letters of his name; people say they are not initials. His friends call him "Rule."

*The Ass-Pocket of Whiskey*, title of Burnside's album recorded with the Jon Spenser Group. Refers to the half-pint of whiskey, which easily fits into the back pocket. You're able to bring your personal party wherever you go, and also leave with it.

VOYEUR and OFFERING TO OSHUN AT THE 55 CLUB

*Oshun*, from the Yoruba belief system is the Orisha (goddess) of feminine sexuality and beauty. Appeals in matters of the heart are made to her.

(NOT IN THE RAP SHEET OR THE OBITUARY)

*Glock*, a 9-millimeter semi-automatic pistol manufactured by Glock.

PRAYER TO SAINT JAMES BYRD OF JASPER, TEXAS
*James Byrd*, lynching victim, dragged to his death behind a pick-up truck in Jasper, Texas.

Gary Copeland Lilley is originally from Sandy Cross, North Carolina, and was a longtime resident of Washington, D.C., where he was a founding member of the Black Rooster Collective. He received the D.C. Commission on the Arts Fellowship for Poetry in 1996 and again in 2000, and he earned a Master of Fine Arts in Poetry from Warren Wilson College in 2002. *The Subsequent Blues* is his first book. He currently lives in Chicago, Illinois.